# The Story of Father Christmas

GW01606025

by

ANN & DENNIS MALLET

Sackett & Marshall Ltd.
London

On Christmas Eve, when you are tucked up in bed, and are too excited to sleep because tomorrow is Christmas Day, and you know that Father Christmas will come in the night and fill your stocking with toys and leave parcels round the Christmas tree, have you ever wondered about Father Christmas himself?

Have you ever wondered how he manages
to land the sledge on the roof and climb down
the chimney with a sack of toys on his back?

Or how he can get into a house with no chimneys to visit the children who live in blocks of flats?

None of us knows for certain the answer to any of these questions, because most of the wonderful things Father Christmas does cannot be explained. They are part of his magic . . . but I will tell you all I know about him, and how he lives, and how he prepares for Christmas all through the year.

I expect you all know what Father Christmas looks like – but in case you do not, he is a large, happy, fat man, with a red face and kind, beaming eyes – and he is always smiling or laughing. His hair is silvery-white, and he has a splendid white moustache and beard. He wears a red cap and tunic, both trimmed with white fur, a black leather belt with a big buckle and a pair of baggy red trousers tucked into black leather boots.

Father Christmas lives far away in the mountains, where the snow lies for most of the year. His house is in a small valley and is made of logs that have been cut from fir trees in forests around the foot of the mountains.

It is a very cosy house, with a high, sloping roof, so that the snow can drain off easily when it starts melting in the spring.

Beside the house on one side is a very big barn where the reindeer live . . . . .

and there is another even bigger barn on the other side,
which is used as a store-house for toys.

Many of you may think that Father Christmas only works at Christmas time, when he and his team of reindeer carry toys in a big sledge to boys and girls all over the world. This is not so.

All the year round he is preparing for Christmas, except during the month of January when he and his reindeer have a well-earned holiday.

At the beginning of February, Father Christmas has to stock up his store of toys again, and to help him do this,he has all his relations, and all his many friends in the valley, and over the mountains in other valleys all around.

LIST of TOYS

He has to visit each family in turn and order dolls from one house, teddy-bears from another house, rocking-horses from a third house, and steam-engines from yet another, and so on. Each house has one special toy that no one else can make as well.

So Father Christmas goes on his rounds throughout the year, and every night, beside his big warm log fire, he writes in a big book exactly how many toys of every sort will be delivered to his store-house by the first of December.

As soon as Spring comes to the valley the new baby reindeer are born, and when they have grown big enough, Father Christmas takes them into a meadow, puts up some fences of different heights, and starts teaching them to jump.

When they have mastered all the fences, and have learnt to trot and gallop and twist and turn, he harnesses them to a sledge to practise. Soon they can do all these things really well. Then comes the most important thing of all . . .
He teaches them to fly!

This takes many months of daily exercise and training. but by the beginning of November he has chosen his team for Christmas.

Then a new sledge has to be made and painted, and more of his friends have this job to do . . . . .

so that Father Christmas always has plenty of time to devote to planning his Christmas Eve journeys.

These journeys start, as every child knows, as soon as darkness falls on Christmas Eve, and from then until sunrise on Christmas Day, Father Christmas and his team of reindeer fly around delivering toys to children all over the world.
How he manages to do this must remain his secret.

When the journeys are over, and children everywhere are opening their presents, and settling down to a long, happy day with a huge dinner of turkey and plum-pudding and crackers afterwards,

Father Christmas and his reindeer fall into their beds and sleep for a whole day and night.

Their Christmas party is on the night of Boxing Day, when, if you happened to be anywhere near that valley

between the mountains, you would see
coming from every direction towards Father Christmas's house, hundreds of lighted torches carried by all his helpers.

The house would be filled with blazing lights, and you would see great pine tables overflowing with good things to eat and drink; and far into the night you would hear the laughter, the singing and the merriment of Father Christmas's party.